KNOWING YOUR TEMPERAMENTS;
Why do you act the way you do?

JOE WHITE.

Table Of content

CHAPTER ONE

Don't fight it! You were born with it.

A person's temperament is a composite of innate characteristics that subtly influences his behavior. Genes transmit these characteristics. Its attribute alignment (genes) is as random as its eye color, hair color, or body size.

Based on personality traits and formative experiences, a person's temperament determines how they act and portray themselves. The way you respond to events is determined by your temperament, which is consistent. It's a technique for identifying persistent personality features.

Behaviors like sociability (outgoing or timid), emotionality (easy-going or fast to react), activity level (high or low energy), concentration level (focused or quickly distracted), and perseverance are all behavioral qualities that are categorized as temperaments (determined or easily discouraged). These illustrations show a range of typical traits, each of which may be useful under particular conditions. Especially as adults, temperament often doesn't change.

We all have a fundamental temperament that we received from our parents, which includes both strengths and flaws. One frequently ponders why he or she behaves in certain ways. Most people ask, "What should I do to change? My dad is short-tempered, and I find myself prone to be as well, even if it's a habit I don't appreciate." The fact is that you might not be able to let go of it easily because your father's DNA greatly influenced who you are, but there are certain techniques to lessen selecting offenses.

Meanwhile, let's familiarize you with the temperaments in the interim....

CHAPTER TWO

The *sparky* Sanguine;

(The warm, buoyant, lively, and enjoying temperament).

They are extremely gregarious creatures, as are those with the sanguine temperament. They are friendly and the first to offer a handshake, a hug, a pat on the back, or to strike up a chat. Making friends comes naturally to them. True social extroverts have a sanguine disposition.

Sanguine temperament persons have a cheerful outlook on life. They want to enjoy life to the fullest and tend to see the positive side of things. They are more prone to notice the positive aspects of a situation than the negative ones. They consider life to be a thrilling, enjoyable experience.

Out of all the temperaments, the sanguine is the most impulsive. They will act if it seems enjoyable and thrilling and won't think twice about the results.

Sanguines are outstanding communicators. They can communicate their message in a way that many others find difficult. Both as salespeople and motivating speakers, they excel. However, they could not be particularly excellent listeners, which means they might be weak in open communication in interpersonal situations.

Sanguines never stop looking for pleasure. If something is tedious or unpleasant, they could find it difficult to stay focused. Because of this, individuals with a sanguine temperament may change jobs frequently in search of a position that they enjoy. They typically focus on the now rather than the past or the future. They might not be able to learn from their mistakes as quickly since they do not take the past into account. They can also be incapable of planning for the future. A pure Sanguine is unlikely to have long-term objectives or ambitions.

They tend to exaggerate and fabricate fantastic stories. When recounting tales, they embellish. Additionally, they frequently exhibit melodramatic responses to issues and exaggerate their thoughts and ideas even when it is not essential or untrue.

Sanguines depend on their loved ones for ongoing assurance. When it comes to expressing your concern for them, presents are most appreciated. If a sanguine receives a lot of attention, time, and presents, they are more likely to stay in a relationship.

People with this temperament are chatty and will engage in conversation with anyone. When you are with a sanguine person, there is never a quiet second. Being open and frank with strangers and even disclosing their family history makes this risky for kids and teenagers with the sanguine temperament. Never at a loss for words, talks without thinking the majority of the time.

The Sanguines are attention-seekers. If their spouse is not giving them enough attention, they can look for another. They won't cut off their pals if they don't offer them enough attention, but instead, they will start looking for others who will give them the attention they need. People with a sanguine temperament are highly expressive. You'll be able to tell immediately if they are upset or annoyed. They will be animated and effervescent if they are joyful. They find it difficult to act anything other than authentically because of this.

All sanguines display a sense of humor, although it's typically a mild one. They like to smile and laugh, and they want everyone else to join them.

Because they are present-oriented, sanguines are ready to forgive and forget. Additionally, they demand fair treatment. They'll want to be pardoned as readily as they would pardon.

They frequently have strong feelings and aren't shy about expressing them. Additionally, feelings rather than rational ideas rule how he makes decisions.

CHAPTER THREE

The *Rocky* Choleric;

(The hot, quick, active, practical, and strong-willed temperament).
This personality type is prone to snap judgments. They frequently make the right choices. They take action to put things right as soon as possible when a bad decision is made on a rare occurrence. Additionally, if they see anything improper happening, they

are not afraid to correct others. Because they don't care about following social norms, their powerful personalities might occasionally make others feel uneasy. They fix everything that needs fixing if it needs fixing.

People with this personality type prefer to concentrate primarily on the large picture, paying less attention to the small details. To keep moving ahead toward that objective, they want to make quick judgments. They sometimes ignore or overthink elements that are necessary for each target stage as a result of their hurry. The quality of the work they do may suffer as a result of blunders.

The ability to influence and manipulate people is a strong suit of choleric types. They frequently drive those who transgress away by pushing them to the limit. Then they fabricate emotional situations that throw the responsibility on the individual being rejected. This personality type frequently produces fictitious outcomes that provide the impression that objectives have been met and can persist for a considerable amount of time in that dream world. No matter what it takes or who suffers harm, they go above and beyond to achieve their objectives. People who have this personality type are constantly pushing others to be their best. They leave no room for other people to breathe. Results are expected, and they want them constantly! This creates an environment where everyone is busy all of the time. They dislike interruptions and setbacks and prefer a "tough love" setting where criticism focuses mostly on the negative.

They display narcissism; the choleric personality observes high degrees of narcissism because they believe they are the most vital member of the team. They possess creative thoughts, the objectives are determined by them, and they have a wider perspective. They are superior to the average person because of this. If left uncontrolled, a choleric personality can elevate itself to the point where the person thinks there is nothing they could do that is wrong. They play on other people's emotions, won't accept any form of apology, and place the blame for whatever flaws they might pick up on.

CHAPTER FOUR

The *maestro* Melancholy;

(The self-sacrificing, gifted, perfectionist, analytical, sensitive temperament).
If you know individuals with a melancholic temperament, you'd probably notice they express themselves with actions rather than words. Individuals with a melancholic temperament are often guarded. Because of

this, they are not likely to express love verbally or emotionally. They instead show their love and affection by being dependable and reliable, and by doing thoughtful things for the people they care about.

Melancholic people naturally lean toward being analytical and intellectual. They often foresee the result of a project long before its completion. They can view situations and problems from all sides and see every possible outcome, unlike the Choleric who rarely anticipates problems or difficulties. This makes them (the Melancholy), very effective at problem-solving, planning, and organizing.

Although people with a melancholic temperament generally keep their emotions guarded, they are still emotional individuals. They may be the most emotional of all the temperament types. Their heightened, ever-changing emotions can result in quick shifts in mood. For instance, they might feel a strong sense of elation and energy, quickly replaced by gloom if something negative happens. By nature, Melancholy is prone to be an introvert, but since his feelings predominate, he is given over to several moods. Most times, their moods will lift him to heights of ecstasy that cause him to act more extroverted, other times, he's so gloomy and depressed, and during these times, he secludes himself and can be very antagonistic.

Due to their introversion, persons with Melancholy temperaments frequently prioritize tasks above interpersonal relationships. This temperamental type enjoys having a list of tasks to fulfill. They could never become inactive. They like to keep themselves busy and like crossing things off of their daily to-do list. In any field, they frequently exhibit exceptional efficiency and productivity. They want to be successful personally since it is highly important to them. Melancholics are often perfectionists and like to do things a certain way. They have a specific idea of the perfect situation, the perfect way to do things, and the perfect outcome. They tend to set incredibly high standards for themselves and others. They pressure themselves to do very well. When the perfect outcome is not achieved, they can become angered; however, these individuals don't typically show their anger until it becomes so pent up over time that they reach a breaking point.

A passionate commitment to friends, family, coworkers and employers is a trait of the melancholy temperament. Loyalty and love attachments must be earned for melancholics, but once they are, they remain faithful for the rest of their lives. To those they respect and who they trust, they are willing to commit and make commitments. They regularly live up to or beyond the expectations of those who matter to them the most. Melancholics have a strong sense of self-motivation since they have a natural tendency toward excellence. Their high standards serve as their primary source of motivation, rather than gifts or the prospect of punishment. They appreciate getting several chances to finish the same activities because they want to get better with each go. Their drive comes from their commitment to giving it their all, and they might get dejected when they don't succeed.

Because they are analytical and fastidious by nature, melancholics are aware of their limitations. Rarely will a melancholic individual take on more than they can handle. They are fully aware of their abilities and limitations. They aren't scared to speak up and be upfront about their incapacity to finish a work or project when asked to go beyond their comfort zones. They are virtually always able to fulfill deadlines because of this attribute.

Despite his or her intense internal feelings, calm and silent. These people frequently decide to conceal their emotions, choosing to keep a level head even in situations that would otherwise cause others to experience intense delight or rage. However, if melancholics are pushed too hard or for too long, they could struggle to maintain control of their anger.

Melancholics prefer predictable routines over shocks and feel most at ease with them. Unexpected occurrences or abrupt changes in routine might upset them and lead to emotional outbursts. These people frequently seem comfortable with the routine of daily life and have no desire to live any other way.

Melancholic people are frequently highly creative, and they frequently address challenges creatively. They have a reputation for being creative in all facets of their lives and for thinking beyond the box. They think of inventive methods to show others how much they care about them, as well as fresh approaches to solving challenging workplace issues.

CHAPTER FIVE

The *flip* Phlegmatic;

(The calm, cool, slow, easy-going, well-balanced temperament).

People with phlegmatic personalities have a strong feeling of obligation to act morally. This takes many different forms. For instance, helping out at a charity store or giving money to the needy. They hope for a more equitable society for all people and find it difficult to comprehend why injustices happen, yet, unlike the Choleric, they may not always take action or show courage in pursuing justice.

is perhaps timid

Phlegmatic personality types don't dance on the tables at Corfu's bars. You'll probably believe they're pretty reserved and unassuming when you first meet one. This is so because they frequently exhibit a state of peace and relaxation. They like abiding by the rules.

In a tragic meaning of the phrase, phlegmatic types are not loners. They desire to have lovely families and fulfilling relationships, which they frequently do. However, they do require some solitude. On their birthday, a sizable surprise party won't go down well. However, they would enjoy a night out with a few close pals.

Phlegmatic types are sympathetic; in addition to feeling empathy, they are curious about other people's worst thoughts. This is done so that they can fully understand what you are going through. They will make an effort to comprehend your experiences so they may assist you better. Because they are so empathetic, they experience other people's suffering more keenly and, as a result, tend to hold themselves responsible when things go wrong. They feel guilty because they were powerless to alleviate that suffering. They are already responsible individuals, but when you add a sense of obligation, empathy, and the desire to assist to the equation, they will inevitably assign blame to themselves.

You won't find a phlegmatic type leading a rebel cause or yelling in a picket line since they tend to follow authority. They respect authority and the values it upholds. Additionally, they find it extremely difficult to breach the law. These people won't have experimented with drugs or smoked marijuana in their childhood. Additionally, they don't fully understand those who have.

They avoid controversy; Because they desire a peaceful society, you won't find them embroiled in a contentious debate. That's a falsehood, in actuality. They'll be the ones attempting to arbitrate and break it up, not you. They won't be the ones starting the fight in the first place, for sure.

They can be indecisive; those who tend to blindly obey authority figures frequently choose to hand off the big choices to others. One such person has a phlegmatic personality type. This is due to several factors, including the fact that their talents lay in the emotional welfare of others and their desire to avoid making the wrong choice for fear of upsetting anybody. They want to focus on that, after all.

In conclusion, a person with a phlegmatic personality type is calm, considerate, and considerate of others. Even if doing so puts their future at risk, they are delighted to aid others.

CHAPTER SIX

THE BLENDED TEMPERAMENT; The various "TEMPERAMENT COMBINATIONS".

Even if one temperament is predominant, having a mixed temperament is a reality.

The several temperament combinations and what they resemble when combined are listed below. You are then prepared to examine how the two temperaments combine once you have determined your "primary temperament" and the temperament that comes in a close second for you.

Your "primary temperament" will be listed first when looking at the different temperament options below. For instance, if your primary temperament is Sanguine and your runner-up temperament is
Choleric, they would be listed as "San/Chol" under the heading "Sanguine" rather than "Chol/San" under the heading "Choleric" (your secondary temperament).

San/Chol – Because both of the basic types are extroverted, this mix is the strongest "extrovert" of all the blends. They are outgoing and exuberant, yet the choleric's determination tempers the sanguine's disorganization. He excels at sales and is almost usually a sports fan. When threatened, he may be annoying and say too much. Without realizing it, the Sanguine's forgetfulness and the Choleric's caustic deposition can harm.

San/Mel – They are extremely emotional people whose moods can change swiftly from highs to lows. The Melancholy's critical temperament can often come out too freely because of the Sanguine's extroverted personality. The greatest way for San/Mel to reach their potential is to collaborate with others because it is quite simple for them to "get down" on themselves.

San/Phleg – The courteous Phlegmatic subdues the Sanguine's brash, outspoken attitude. These are incredibly joyful, cheerful folks that love to serve others. Although they would never intentionally injure someone, they struggle with a lack of workplace drive and would much prefer to go on vacation than work.

CHOLERIC
Chol/San – The second most powerful extrovert is a driven, busy person with a lot of energy. He is nearly fearless. No matter what he does, his mind is constantly engaged and working. His flaws blend the bitterness of the Choleric with the savage rage of the Sanguine. Ulcers are both something he gets and gives. Because of his explosive temper, he could leave others (including his spouse and children) shaken and resentful.

Chol/Mel – The Choleric/Melancholy is a very talented and diligent person. He works hard and pays attention to detail. He is verbally confrontational while also paying close attention to details. He is aggressive and very competitive. He tends to be authoritarian and opinionated, working meticulously until the task is accomplished. Due to the perfectionist tendencies of the Melancholy and the Choleric, he has trouble getting along with other people.

Chol/Phleg – The quietest of the extroverted temperaments is this one. Though first, he may not seem impressive, he is ultimately quite adept. He is methodical and a skilled planner. Because he always considers how he may engage others to assist him, he frequently accomplishes more than people with other temperaments. His flaws include a propensity to stifle his resentment rather than express it. He finds it challenging to own his flaws, and he frequently worries about how he performs in daily tasks.

PHLEGMATIC
Phlegm/San – Being kind, joyful, and people-focused makes this the easiest to get along with.
They are good candidates for administrative positions and other occupations requiring interpersonal skills. He might not be motivated or disciplined, and he might perform below his full potential. Years may pass as he "putters around" with no forward movement.

Phlegm/Chol – Although he is the most active introvert, he will never be a fireball. He is a good listener, which makes him a great counselor. He is helpful, realistic, and patient. If threatened, he could lack drive and turn obstinate. He can also have a propensity for passivity and inactivity. He needs social interaction since he is an externally motivated person.

Phlegm/Mel – This is kind and peaceful, acts honorably, and is trustworthy. He oscillates between being forgiving and critical, and he could lean toward negativity. They could resist joining a group because they are concerned about overcommitting themselves.

MELANCHOLY
Mel/San – They are ordered and precise, and the Sanguine's friendly and gregarious nature helps to moderate the Melancholy. His structured side is knowledgeable about the facts, and his sanguine side makes him engaging to listen to, therefore he makes a great instructor. If he enters the sales field, it will be sales that need meticulous attention to detail and the presentation of numerous data.

He has a wide range of emotions, from being moved to tears to being harsh and judgmental of others. Both temperaments have the potential to be afraid, which might result in an insecure individual with a negative self-perception.

Mel/Chol – This perfectionism and desire may lead him to a career in law or medicine. They combine drive and decisiveness. They may be quite challenging to satisfy because of the melancholy's critical character. If they start feeling bad about someone or something, it will probably be with them for a while. Their combined traits may cause individuals to criticize others and seek retribution from those they quarrel with.

Mel/Phleg - These are frequently academics and teachers. They combine order and analysis and are less likely to become hostile than other gloomy mixtures. They are great bookkeepers and accountants. Unfortunately, he is prone to discouragement and could experience dread and worry. Due to their tendency for being inflexible and stubborn, they could become uncooperative.

CHAPTER SEVEN

Occupational description for the different temperaments.

SANGUINES:

They make good salespeople and sales representatives, healthcare workers, instructors, conversationalists, public speakers, and on occasion, good leaders.

Sanguine women are never reasonable in anything. They should pick professions that provide them with a lot of opportunities to interact with others.

CHOLERICS:

Cholerics make effective bosses, producers, tyrants, criminals (depending on their moral stance), and businessmen.

Though he is far less emotional, the choleric also makes a fine preacher. The world has profited and suffered from the choleric; they have been the great generals, rulers, and gangsters of the planet. Their objectives and moral standards made a difference.

MELANCHOLICS:
The majority of the world's greatest composers, painters, musicians, inventors, theologians, philosophers, educators, and theorists have been melancholics. Consider the works of Rembrandt, Van Gogh, Beethoven, Mozart, and several more artists. They are also skilled at becoming scientists, engineers, artisans, and other vocations that benefit humanity.

PHLEGMATICS:
The world of education tends to appeal to phlegmatics. Teachers at primary schools tend to be phlegmatic. The only people with the patience to teach a class of first-graders to read are they. A sanguine would tell the kids stories throughout the lesson. They

would fear reading aloud because sadness would judge them so harshly. Could you see a choleric teaching first grade? The kids might want to run out the windows! The phlegmatic's soft disposition ensures the best environment for such learning.

They are also skilled in precise jobs like accounting and diplomacy.

www.ingramcontent.com/pod-product-compliance
Lightning Source LLC
Chambersburg PA
CBHW070224180726
47999CB00017B/2305